Landmark
Events in
American
History

The Transcontinental
Railroad

Michael V. Uschan

WORLD ALMANAC® LIBRARY

Please visit our web site at: www.worldalmanaclibrary.com
For a free color catalog describing World Almanac® Library's list of high-quality
books and multimedia programs, call 1-800-848-2928 (USA) or 1-800-387-3178
(Canada). World Almanac® Library's fax: (414) 332-3567.

Library of Congress Cataloging-in-Publication Data

Uschan, Michael V., 1948-
    The transcontinental railroad / by Michael V. Uschan.
       p. cm. — (Landmark events in American history)
    Summary: Discusses the history of railroads in the United States, focusing on the
construction of the Transcontinental Railroad. Includes relevant historical quotations.
    Includes bibliographical references and index.
    ISBN 0-8368-5382-2 (lib. bdg.)
    ISBN 0-8368-5410-1 (softcover)
    1. Pacific railroads—Juvenile literature. 2. Railroads—History—Juvenile literature.
[1. Pacific railroads. 2. Railroads—History.] I. Title. II. Series.
    TF25.P2U83   2003
    385'.0979—dc21   2003049709

First published in 2004 by
World Almanac® Library
330 West Olive Street, Suite 100
Milwaukee, WI 53212 USA

Produced by Discovery Books
Editor: Sabrina Crewe
Designer and page production: Sabine Beaupré
Photo researcher: Sabrina Crewe
Maps and diagrams: Stefan Chabluk
World Almanac® Library editorial direction: Mark J. Sachner
World Almanac® Library art direction: Tammy Gruenewald
World Almanac® Library production: Beth Meinholz and Jessica Yanke

Photo credits: California Historical Society: p. 14; Iris and B. Gerald Cantor Center for
Visual Arts, Stanford University, gift of David Hewes: p. 31; Central Pacific Railroad
Photographic History Museum (CPRR.org): pp. 4, 5, 10, 19, 21, 22, 27, 32; Corbis: cover,
pp. 6, 11, 13, 16, 24, 25, 26, 28, 30, 33, 36, 42; The Granger Collection: p. 38; North
Wind Picture Archives: pp. 7, 8, 9, 12, 15, 17, 18, 20, 23, 29, 34, 35, 37, 39, 40, 43.

Printed in the United States of America

Contents

Introduction

The **Transcontinental** Railroad was the first railroad to span the western United States. It was also the biggest, most complex construction project undertaken in the nineteenth century. The suitably named George Francis Train, who helped raise money for the project, dramatically proclaimed it "the grandest enterprise under God!" The railroad actually only crossed the western half of the continent, but it was called the Transcontinental Railroad because it enabled travel from one side of the continent to the other by linking with existing railroads in the East.

Two Railroads

The Transcontinental Railroad was a joint project of two railroad companies that, in the 1860s, became the nation's biggest and richest companies. The Union Pacific Railroad built 1,086 miles (1,747 kilometers) of track west from Omaha, Nebraska. The Central Pacific

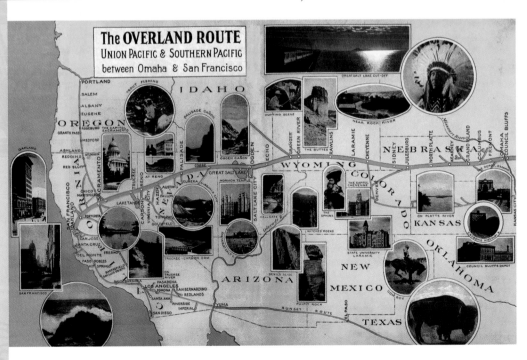

This map was drawn in 1908 and shows places of interest along the Transcontinental Railroad. By 1908, the Central Pacific Railroad had changed its name to the Southern Pacific, as it is called here, and the route reached all the way to the Pacific coast at San Francisco.

constructed 689 miles (1,109 km) of railroad east from Sacramento, California. On May 10, 1869, they linked their lines at Promontory Summit in Utah to complete the nation's first transcontinental railroad.

A Difficult Project

Building this huge railroad required laying track over some of North America's most desolate, dangerous, and difficult terrain. The Transcontinental Railroad would snake through vast areas of inhospitable desert, cross swift rivers and deep canyons, and hurdle towering, snow-capped mountains. When there was no other possible route, it would cut right through mountains via tunnels, sometimes blasted out of solid rock with explosives.

It took more than six years, from 1863 to 1869, to build the Transcontinental Railroad. It required the heroic labors of some twenty thousand workers, a few of whom died while attempting a task many thought impossible. Some of those lives were lost in battles with Native people, who fought the railroad's coming because its tracks crossed their territory and would destroy their way of life.

A Valuable Connection

The railroad was fantastically expensive, costing hundreds of millions of dollars in an era when most people earned only a few dollars a week. The Transcontinental Railroad, however, would finally connect the two halves of a nation that was rapidly expanding on each side of the vast North American continent. The quick, easy, and affordable means of transportation of people and products that the Transcontinental Railroad provided would help the United States grow richer and expand its borders.

Workers start to make a tunnel in a sheer rock face. In the days before machinery, much of the work was done by hand with picks and shovels, and the rock was then removed on small carts.

Chapter 1

A Growing Nation

The First Railroads

Railroads were first built in European mines in the sixteenth century, and the first **trains** were pulled by either men or horses. In the 1820s, in Britain, **locomotives** powered by steam engines began pulling trains.

In 1827, the Baltimore and Ohio Railroad became the first American railroad company. It began operating August 28, 1830, when a locomotive named Tom Thumb made a run from Baltimore, Maryland, to Elicott Mill 13 miles (21 km) away. In 1830, there were only 23 miles (37 km) of track in the United States. By 1835, there were over 1,000 miles (1,600 km), by 1850, an estimated 9,000 miles (14,500 km), and by 1860, over 30,000 miles (48,000 km). All of that track, however, was east of the Mississippi River.

The Atlantic locomotive, shown here, went into operation on the Baltimore and Ohio Railroad in the summer of 1832. It is pulling two double-decker carriages converted from stagecoaches.

Traveling West

If people wanted to travel from the East to California before the Transcontinental Railroad was built, the journey took months. It entailed hardships and dangers that made the trip difficult to endure, sometimes even to survive.

Pioneers traveling in wagons perished from illness, from lack of water or food, or in battles with Indians in a cross-country trek that could take up to six months. An ocean voyage around Cape Horn in South America also took months. The journey could be shortened by crossing Panama in Central America, but that route was so expensive that most people could not afford it. Also, people who went across Panama often contracted yellow fever and other diseases that made them ill and sometimes killed them.

Rapid Growth

The original thirteen British colonies that united as the United States in 1776 were in the East, but the new nation had gradually

Crossing the continent to take supplies west, a group of travelers struggles against a snowstorm. Before the railroad crossed the country, the journey from east to west took several months.

Everyone Wants a Railroad

"The sunburned immigrant, walking with his wife and little ones beside his gaunt and weary oxen in mid-continent, the sea-sick traveler, the homesick bride whose wedding trip had included a passage of the 'Isthmus' [Panama], the merchant whose stock needed replenishing, everyone prayed for a Pacific railroad."

Hubert Howe Bancroft, nineteenth-century historian

expanded to claim land west, all the way to the Pacific Ocean. By the middle of the nineteenth century, the United States was growing rapidly on both North American coasts.

In 1848, the United States won the Mexican War and gained possession of the Mexican province of California, as well as Texas and land in the Southwest. That same year, gold was discovered in California, touching off a mad dash for riches that brought hundreds of thousands of people there in just a few years. Settlers were also flocking west to the fertile land of Oregon, another U.S. possession.

Thousands of people came to California in the early 1850s to hunt for gold. Many stayed after the Gold Rush, and California became increasingly important to the rest of the United States.

Pushing Out the Native Population

In the mid-nineteenth century, the nation's two main population centers, east and west, were separated by a vast territory in between. Although white settlement had pushed westward from the East, the center of the continent had not yet been taken over by white people and was inhabited by Native peoples. These peoples comprised both the original inhabitants of the central region and tribes that had been pushed out of their homelands in other areas.

For Native people, the region was the last refuge from white settlers. For white Americans, it was a geographical block to communication and transportation between two centers of population. The United States wanted to find an easier, faster way to move people and products across the vast expanse of land it had claimed for its nation.

A Possible Solution

In the 1830s, people began to talk about a transcontinental railroad. One early champion of this idea was New York City businessman Asa Whitney, who tried for years to convince U.S. officials to build the railroad. By 1851, California, feeling cut off from the rest of the nation, had become the project's strongest supporter.

Stagecoaches and the Pony Express

Before the Transcontinental Railroad, other services had provided communication links and transportation between America's two coasts. On September 16, 1858, John Butterfield began a stagecoach line from Tipton, Missouri, to San Francisco. His "swift wagons" cut the time of the 1,800-mile (2,900-km) trip from several months to twenty-five days.

On April 3, 1860, the daring riders of the Pony

Each Pony Express rider rode 75–125 miles (120–200 km) before handing over the mail to the next messenger at a station on the route.

Express began delivering mail to the West. These lone horsemen carried letters from Missouri to California quicker than Butterfield's wagons did—the record run was seven days and sixteen hours to deliver the text of President Abraham Lincoln's inaugural address in 1861. On October 24, 1861, the Pony Express became **obsolete** when the Pacific **Telegraph** Company and the Overland Telegraph Company jointly completed the first transcontinental telegraph line. Messages could now be sent in hours rather than days.

Backers claimed that cutting the time it took to cross the continent would help the United States become richer and stronger. It would make it easier to do business with Asian countries such as China; goods could be carried by rail to California and then sent overseas on ships. A transcontinental railroad would also increase communication, travel, and commerce between the eastern and western sections of the United States.

There would be another benefit from the railroad. It would help Americans achieve their most cherished goal—**Manifest** Destiny.

In 1849, Asa Whitney produced this map to promote interest in a transcontinental railroad. Presented to Congress, the map suggested a number of possible routes, shown by the darkest lines running across the western two-thirds of the continent.

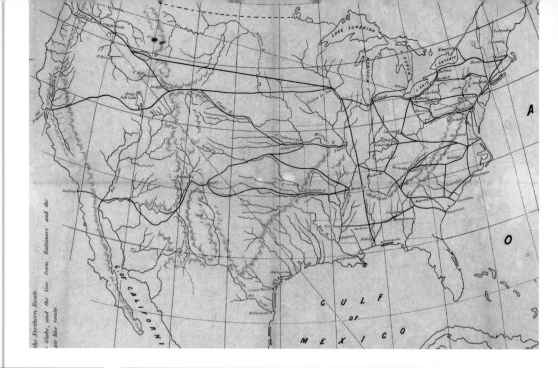

A Great National Highway

"A Railroad, from some point on the Mississippi, or its tributaries, to some point on the bay of San Francisco, is the best route that can be adopted for the purpose of securing the Commerce of China and India; . . . to open a great national highway from California to the Atlantic coast, would be a greater defense and protection than all other military works. . . . It is the duty of this Legislature to encourage the speedy building of a Railroad from the Atlantic to the Pacific, across the territory of the United States."

J. J. Warner, Report on Railroads to the Senate of California, 1851

Asa Whitney (1797—1872)

One of the first people to propose a transcontinental railroad was Asa Whitney, who was born in Connecticut. He was a businessman who became rich by buying and selling products in China and other Asian countries, and he lived in China from 1842 to 1844. Whitney began a long crusade to persuade government officials that a railroad that crossed the continent would help the United States become more powerful. Whitney toured the country between 1844 and 1851, giving speeches urging the construction of a railroad from Chicago to the Pacific. He also suggested a plan to the British, who then controlled Canada, for a Canadian transcontinental railroad. Whitney finally gave up in 1852. Although he failed in his quest to build the railroad, Whitney made many people realize how important transportation between east and west would be to the country's future.

Manifest Destiny

Many white Americans believed it was their right and destiny to rule all the land between the Atlantic and Pacific Oceans. This belief was expressed as the ideal of "Manifest Destiny." In the 1850s, people such as Missouri Senator Thomas Hart Benton realized that a transcontinental railroad could help Manifest Destiny become reality by making it easier for people to move west and settle new areas. Said Benton: "Emigrants would flock upon it as pigeons to their roosts [and carry west] all that civilization affords to enliven the wild domain from the Mississippi to the Pacific."

Manifest Destiny was the underlying reason Americans wanted to build the first railroad to reach the West. Many people, however, had trouble believing such a huge and difficult project could be accomplished.

In this painting, the woman floating westward over the prairie, while Indians flee, symbolizes Manifest Destiny and progress as envisaged by white Americans. She holds a book and telegraph wire to represent education and communication.

Making Plans

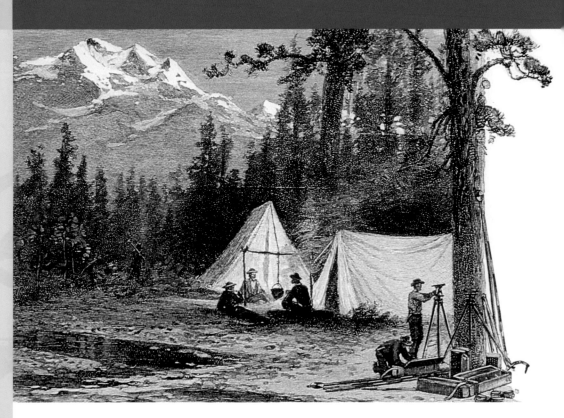

The U.S. Army's team of engineers explored the West in the 1850s, looking for a possible route for a railroad. This engraving shows one group's camp in the Rocky Mountains.

Searching for a Route

As the population in the West grew in the late 1840s and early 1850s, so did support for a railroad to connect the two halves of the nation. On March 3, 1853, therefore, Congress directed Secretary of War Jefferson Davis to map a route from the Mississippi River to the Pacific Ocean.

Over three years, teams of the Army Corps of **Topographical** Engineers roamed 4,000 square miles (10,000 square kilometers) of the West. Their exploration yielded five possible routes. The routes had eastern starting points as far apart as St. Paul, Minnesota, and Fort Smith, Arkansas, and western terminals ranging from Seattle, Washington, to Los Angeles, California.

The teams, however, failed to discover a path over the Sierra Nevada, the mountain range (*sierra* means "mountain range" in Spanish) that formed a towering barrier to the West. This task would be left to a young engineer with the nickname of "Crazy Judah."

Crazy Judah

In 1854, Theodore Judah had come to Sacramento, California, to survey a route for a small railroad. Judah stayed to work on other projects and became obsessed with discovering a path over the Sierra Nevada. His passion to build a transcontinental railroad was intense, which is why people began calling him "Crazy Judah."

In the fall of 1860, Judah—together with Daniel "Doc" Strong, a pharmacist from the small mining town of Dutch Flat—finally discovered a way over the rugged mountains. The route climbed eastward from a plateau between California's American and Yuba Rivers to Donner **Pass**. From there, the route angled down to the Truckee River valley and the Nevada desert.

A Report to Congress

"Although the importance of such a work to the prosperity of the nation cannot be doubted, there is reason to suppose that many years will elapse before the resources of the country will be found sufficient for its accomplishment. The natural obstacles to be overcome are the Rocky Mountains and the Sierra Nevada, the deserts between the Missouri and the former chain, and those of the great basin, the flying sands, and the want of timber."

Report of the Superintendent of the Census to the House of Representatives, December 1, 1851

Snow covers the Sierra Nevada at Donner Pass, named after the leader of a group of travelers who died there in the winter of 1846 to 1847. The road that goes through Donner Pass today, visible in this photograph, is part of Interstate 80.

The Big Four

Realizing the railroad was now possible, Judah began recruiting California businesspeople to invest in it. In 1861, his efforts led seven men to start the Central Pacific Railroad. The richest and most powerful among them were known as the "Big Four": Collis Huntington, Mark Hopkins, Charles Crocker, and Leland Stanford, the railroad's president. Stanford was also elected governor of California on September 4, 1861.

Theodore Dehone Judah (1826—1863)

Theodore Dehone Judah was born in Bridgeport, Connecticut, and studied engineering in New York. He worked on a number of canal construction projects before turning to railroad engineering.

Judah was working for the Sacramento Valley Railroad when he became enthusiastic about building a railroad across the Sierra Nevada. He found a path over the range, brought together backers for the Central Pacific, and became the company's chief engineer. Judah even helped win support from the **federal** government.

Although responsible for creating the Transcontinental Railroad, Judah never lived to see his great dream realized. In October 1863, he left for New York to raise money and gather support for the railroad. Judah headed south by ship, still the quickest way to travel between the two coasts. Then, while crossing Panama, he caught yellow fever and died a week after reaching New York.

The Battle Over Routes

Judah's discovery had removed one of the last barriers to building a transcontinental railroad. Another obstacle to its construction disappeared in 1861, when the Civil War began.

Ever since the Army Corps had mapped possible routes for the railroad, officials from northern and southern states had waged a political battle over where its eastern starting point should be. Both regions wanted it to be in one of their states because they believed their region would then become stronger and richer than the other. The argument caused delays.

The Pacific Railway Act

When the Civil War started, however, the U.S. government decided to go ahead with the project along a northern route. President Abraham Lincoln and other leaders believed the nation needed the railroad more than ever to strengthen its bond with its western territories in a time of civil war.

On July 1, 1862, Lincoln signed the Pacific Railway Act. The legislation authorized construction of the Transcontinental Railroad

Three of the Central Pacific's "Big Four" are seen in this portrait of railroad chiefs. It also shows the Ames brothers and Sidney Dillon, who were involved in the Union Pacific, and D. H. Moffat, a supporter of the railroad.

Worth Every Penny

"I would sink a hundred million dollars in opening a railroad and do it most cheerfully, and think I had done a great thing for my country. What are seventy-five or a hundred million dollars in opening a railroad across the central regions of this continent that shall connect the people of the Atlantic and Pacific and bind us together? Nothing."

Senator Henry Wilson of Massachusetts, Senate debate on the Pacific Railway Act, 1862

Sacramento was chosen as the western starting point for the Transcontinental Railroad. The town had sprung up only a few years earlier near the site of California's first large gold discovery, but it soon became the state capital.

by two companies: the Union Pacific Railroad and the Central Pacific Railroad. The Central Pacific would lay track east from Sacramento, and the Union Pacific would head west from a point still to be decided. They would connect their lines at a spot to be determined later. The Act also authorized the government to grant the two railroads low-**interest** loans for each mile of track they laid.

Leland Stanford (1824—1893)

Leland Stanford was born in New York and trained to be a lawyer. After practicing law for just a few years, Stanford headed west in 1852 to join his brothers, who had set up a business selling goods during the Gold Rush. He became a successful merchant in Sacramento and ran for governor in 1859 and 1861, winning the second time. A staunch Republican, Stanford made sure California stayed loyal to the United States during the Civil War.

When Theodore Judah persuaded him to support the building of a railroad, Stanford threw himself into the enterprise, becoming—and remaining for the rest of his life—the leading figure of the Central Pacific Railroad. As governor, he gave a lot of state support to the project. In 1885, years after the railroad was completed, Stanford (by then a U.S. senator) made another huge contribution to California when he and his wife founded Stanford University at Palo Alto. Stanford is now one of the nation's top schools.

A New Partnership

The railroad's enormous size and the expense of its construction necessitated a bold new relationship between business and government, one in which they became partners. It was the first time the federal government worked with private companies to accomplish such a great task.

William Tecumseh Sherman, an army officer who had become famous as a Civil War general, once noted there was no other way to fund such a huge endeavor. In a letter to his brother, a congressman, Sherman called the Transcontinental Railroad "a work of giants" and claimed, "Uncle Sam is the only giant I know who can [handle] the subject."

From Omaha to Sacramento

The Pacific Railway Act appointed President Lincoln to choose the railroad's eastern starting point. In 1863, therefore, after much consideration, President Lincoln selected Omaha, a city in Nebraska Territory. Construction could finally begin on the most challenging construction project in U.S. history.

Omaha, Nebraska, was the eastern starting point of the Transcontinental Railroad. From there, a number of railroads would connect passengers to the East.

Chapter 3

Building the Railroad

Workers on both the Union Pacific and the Central Pacific had to work in deep snow. Sometimes the railroad they were building became buried, like this one in Colorado, and they had to dig down deep to reach it.

The Anvil Chorus
"It is a grand 'Anvil Chorus' that the sturdy sledges are playing across the plains. It is in triple time, three strokes to the spike. There are 10 spikes to a rail, 40 rails to a mile, 1,800 miles to San Francisco—21 million times are those sledges to be swung, 21 million times are they to come down with their sharp punctuation before the great work of modern America is complete."

Newspaper report on Union Pacific construction, 1866

The Central Pacific

Building the Transcontinental Railroad would not be easy. Workers would have to lay track over mountains that soared thousands of feet high. They would have to toil in bone-chilling mountain cold and blazing desert heat. And they would have to survive conflicts with Native peoples, who wanted to stop Americans from invading their homeland with the "iron horse."

The Central Pacific was the first to begin work. On January 8, 1863, Leland Stanford, the Central Pacific's president and governor of California, tipped a ceremonial shovel of sand onto a Sacramento street to begin construction.

The Central Pacific had to lay track over the railroad's most difficult stretch, the mountains of the Sierra Nevada. But construction was slow even before workers got to the range, which began 128 miles (206 km) east of Sacramento. The first rail of the Central Pacific was not laid until October 26, 1863, and it took until the end of the following February to lay the first 18 miles (29 km) of track.

There were reasons for the lack of progress. The Civil War slowed construction by consuming available manpower—because the war needed thousands of men for soldiers—as well as building materials, horses, and supplies. The Central Pacific also had long waits for what equipment it could get from the East. The materials had to be transported on ships, and the voyages took months.

When equipment arrived, it was taken by wagon to sites along the railroad route. This wagon train carrying railroad supplies was photographed near Cisco in California.

Laying the Railroad

Workers first had to **grade** the roadbed the tracks would run on. Then they put down a bed of wooden ties, the heavy wooden blocks that connected the rails and held them in place. Once the roadbed was prepared, it was time to lay down the line of iron rails the trains would run on. The rails were brought forward on cars over track already laid. A group of men would lift an iron rail, carry it swiftly to its spot on the track, and drop it into place, a process that took only thirty seconds. When the rail was down, workers with sledgehammers would begin pounding ten spikes through each rail. Each spike would bind the rail to the tie beneath it and then anchor it into the ground. Workers would pound each spike home with three swings that rang out loud when they hit, and then they would move on to the next spike.

The only way to get the railroad past Cape Horn was to cut a zigzagging route into its steep side. This photograph was taken during construction from a train on Cape Horn looking down to the American River far below.

Over the Mountains

The Central Pacific did not reach the mountains until 1866, after which the pace slackened further. Even on a flat surface, laying railroad track was slow, backbreaking labor. This process was much more difficult in the Sierra Nevada, through which Judah had mapped a twisting, up-and-down, 100-mile (160-km) path. To lay track, workers had to blast roadbeds out of solid rock, sometimes making tunnels that went straight through a mountain.

The first major obstacle was Cape Horn, a cliff towering 1,000 feet (300 meters) over the American River. To cut a railroad into its side, workers had to be lowered down the cliff face in baskets. They drilled holes and filled them with blasting powder. After lighting fuses, the men were pulled up to safety before the powder exploded and tore a huge chunk of rock out of the mountain. Workers then carried the debris away in baskets and smoothed a flat surface with pickaxes, sledgehammers, and shovels.

Dangerous Conditions

The path that Central Pacific workers carved through the Sierra Nevada included fifteen tunnels with a total length of 6,213 feet (1,894 m). The work was dangerous—the explosives sometimes

Summit, at 1,659 feet (506 m), was the longest tunnel the railroad workers built in the Sierra Nevada. This is a view inside Summit Tunnel before the track was laid.

ignited too quickly and killed tunnel laborers. This was especially true when the Central Pacific began using nitroglycerin, a new, more powerful explosive that was so volatile it sometimes detonated accidentally all by itself.

Cold and heavy snow also made life difficult and dangerous. During the winter of 1866–1867, forty-four blizzards slowed down the pace of construction to an average of only 8 inches (20 centimeters) of new track a day. The snows grew so deep—40 feet (12 m) in some places—that half the workers were kept busy shoveling snow so construction could continue. There were also avalanches that killed workers and destroyed supplies.

Picking up Speed

The Central Pacific did not complete the mountain route until April 3, 1868, when it reached Truckee, California, on the Sierra Nevada's east side. But the railroad's pace then picked up, as it swiftly began laying track through the flat desert of Nevada and into Utah Territory. In 1868 alone, the Central Pacific laid 360 miles (580 km) of track as it pushed east to meet the Union Pacific.

A Deadly Avalanche

"Snowslides or avalanches were frequent [in the Sierra Nevada]. The storm winds, being always from the southwest, form drifts or snow wreaths on the northeast crests of hills. When these become too heavy they break off, and in falling start the loose snow below [to slide] on the old crust. Near the close of one storm, a log house containing some fifteen or sixteen men in all, was crushed and buried up at day-break. The storm ended at noon. Towards evening a man coming up the road missed the house and alarmed the camp, so that by six o'clock the men were dug out. Only three were killed."

John R. Gilliss, Central Pacific civil engineer

The Union Pacific

It was much easier to lay track on the Union Pacific route. The Transcontinental Railroad runs in an almost straight line between Sacramento and Omaha, and the Union Pacific line was built mostly through the flat **Great Plains.** The Union Pacific route pushed west along the Platte River, crossing through territories that would become the states of Nebraska, Colorado, Wyoming, and Utah.

Although it had the easier route, it took some years for the Union Pacific to get started. The company had been created by the 1862 Railway Act, but it took time to find leaders to run the new company. The Union Pacific's executives first gathered in October 1863 in New York City. Top officers included Thomas Durant, a vice president who first had to raise money to start the company and then oversee construction throughout much of the project.

The Union Pacific building pace was very slow for several years. As with the Central Pacific, the Civil War made it difficult for the Union Pacific to get workers and supplies. The new firm had an additional problem in trying to raise enough money to start construction—under the 1862 Railway Act, neither railroad could receive any federal loans until it had laid some track.

For all these reasons, the Union Pacific did not extend its line beyond the Omaha city limits until July 1865. When the Civil War ended, however, the Union Pacific began laying track more quickly.

Working Song
"Then drill, my Paddies, drill; Drill, my heroes, drill; Drill all day, No sugar in your tay [tea], Workin' on the U. P. Railway."

Lyrics of a song about Irish Union Pacific workers

Building a railroad across the Plains was easier and faster than in the mountains. This print shows a typical busy scene during construction of the Union Pacific somewhere in Nebraska.

This is the original wooden bridge built in 1868 over Dale Creek in Wyoming. It towered 150 feet (46 m) above the creek bed.

Union Pacific Problems

Although the route through the Great Plains was generally flat, the Union Pacific did encounter creeks and rivers, and it had to build many bridges. The longest was a 650-foot (200-m) wooden **trestle** across Dale Creek in Wyoming.

Several weather problems plagued the workers. In summer, desert temperatures soared to 110° F (43° C), and water was scarce. Jack Casement, who was in charge of work crews, wrote his wife about conditions in central Wyoming: "This is an awful place . . . dust knee-deep. We haul all our water 50 miles (80 km) and we're losing a great many mules, six nice fat ones died in less than an hour today."

Native Americans Fight Back

If the building of the railroad was dangerous and difficult for workers, it was a disaster for the Native peoples who lived in its path.

The railroad companies were not just set on running rails through Indian homelands—they were also determined to get rid of the buffalo that roamed the Great Plains. The Plains tribes depended on buffalo hunts for food and to sustain their way of life. Sioux Chief Red Cloud warned Union Pacific officials: "We do not want you here. You are scaring away the buffalo."

The Plains Indians were willing to fight to stop the railroad's invasion of their homeland. They tore up rails, derailed trains by piling logs on tracks, and attacked workers. On August 6, 1867, Cheyenne Chief Turkey Foot and his men derailed a train near Plum Creek, Nebraska, 230 miles (370 km) west of Omaha, and killed several workers.

The Government Responds

Union Pacific chief engineer Grenville Dodge had been a Union Army general during the Civil War. He realized that his men needed protection if the railroad was to be completed. He gave the federal government an ultimatum: "We've got to clean the Indian out, or give up. The government may take its choice."

General Sherman of the U.S. Army promised to act. He even expressed the hope that "not an Indian will be left in that belt of country through which the two railroads pass." Within a few decades, Sherman's words would virtually come true. Meanwhile, government officials ordered the posting of five thousand U.S.

Cheyenne warriors attack a working party on the Transcontinental Railroad in 1867. The situation was so bad, said chief engineer Grenville Dodge, that the workers kept "picks and shovels in one hand, the rifle in the other, and often had to drop one to use the other."

How Workers Lived

After a day of hard labor, Central Pacific and Union Pacific workers needed a place to eat and sleep. The solution was the "**perpetual** train," which followed them down the track they were laying. Pushed rather than pulled by an engine, this train had many specialized cars. Some were devoted to construction needs, such as those that housed blacksmith shops, while others were for workers to sleep and eat in. Sleeping cars were 85 feet (26 m) long and had triple tiers of bunks. Dining cars were big enough to feed 125 men at one time. Every 60 miles (100 km) or so along the route, a temporary town would spring up. These towns had amenities for workers such as a bathhouse and a saloon, where they could drink and gamble. The makeshift communities—nicknamed "Hell on Wheels" because workers got into so much trouble there—were abandoned as workers laid more track and moved away.

soldiers to protect railroad work crews from Indian attacks.

Workers on the Railroad

Railroad workers were called **roustabouts**, **gandy dancers**, and **bridge monkeys**, colorful nicknames that stemmed from the jobs they did. The laborers employed by the two railroads were paid an average of $3 (about $38 today) a day for working twelve-hour shifts, six days a week.

The twenty thousand people who built the railroad came from all over the world. The Central Pacific had trouble recruiting workers until it began hiring the Chinese people who had originally come to California in the 1850s seeking gold. Some people feared that the Chinese, smaller on average than white Americans, would not be strong enough to do the job. They proved to be fine workers, but even so they were paid much less than other workers. The Central Pacific eventually hired over ten thousand Chinese workers, 90 percent of its work force.

A group of Central Pacific workers pose for a photograph on a railroad handcar. The car moved along the track when the handle was pumped up and down.

Indispensable Workers

"The great portion of the laborers employed by us are Chinese, who constitute a large element in the population of California. Without them it would be impossible to complete the western portion of this great national enterprise. As a class they are quiet, peaceable, patient, industrious and economical. Ready and apt to learn all the different kinds of work required in railroad building, they soon become as efficient as white laborers."

Leland Stanford, Central Pacific report to the U.S. government, October 10, 1867

Most Union Pacific workers were soldiers who had fought in the Civil War or immigrants from European countries, mainly Ireland. The Union Pacific also employed several hundred African Americans, many of them former slaves.

The Railroads Compete

As the two railroads got closer to each other, they began to compete to see which could lay track fastest. The main reason was that the more track they laid, the more land and loans they would receive from the federal government. Workers also wanted to be considered the best, and they competed gleefully.

In 1868, the Union Pacific began bragging about having laid a record 4.5 miles (7 km) of track in one day. The Central Pacific then decided to outdo its competitor, and it built 6 miles (10 km) in a single day. When the Union Pacific responded with an 8.5-mile (14-km) effort, Central Pacific cofounder Charles Crocker bet Union Pacific chief Thomas Durant the sum of $10,000 (about

This sign in Utah honors the extraordinary labors of the Central Pacific workers who competed with Union Pacific crews along the last stretches of the Transcontinental Railroad. The sign stands by a now-disused roadbed that is part of the Golden Spike National Historic Site in Utah.

A somewhat fantastical view of work on the Transcontinental Railroad. This woodcut shows workers from both crews on the last mile. In the background, explosives send rocks flying in the air. Workers can be seen hauling away rock, wielding pickaxes, and laying ties.

$125,000 today) that his railroad could not beat that record. Crocker accepted the challenge but waited until the railroads were only 14 miles (23 km) from the point where they would connect. He did not want the Union Pacific to have a chance to regain the record.

On April 28, 1869, more than three thousand Central Pacific laborers started the minute the sun came up at 7:15 A.M. Except for a brief lunch break, they kept working feverishly until 7:00 P.M. When they were finished, they had set in place 10 miles, 56 feet (16 km) of track. To accomplish this amazing feat, workers laid 25,800 wooden ties and 3,520 rails weighing over 560 pounds (254 kilograms) each, and they drove home tens of thousands of spikes.

End of the Line

Three days later, on May 1, 1869, the railroads ran their lines into Promontory Summit in Utah Territory, the site at which the federal government had chosen to unite the Union Pacific and Central Pacific Railroads. The workers left a gap the length of one rail, which the two teams would complete in a ceremony to unite the two halves of the Transcontinental Railroad.

Chapter 4

From Coast to Coast

This photograph was taken at the ceremony on May 10, 1869. It shows workers and officials from both railroad crews clustered around the two locomotives that met where the tracks joined at Promontory Summit.

Ceremonial Connection

On May 10, 1869, a ceremony took place at Promontory Summit, a deserted spot in the wilderness 56 miles (90 km) from the town of Ogden in Utah Territory. There, the Central Pacific and Union Pacific Railroads united their tracks with a large ceremony. In the

A Late Ceremony

The two lines of the Transcontinental Railroad were united on May 10, 1869, but the ceremony had originally been scheduled for May 8. The delay was caused by the kidnapping of Union Pacific official Thomas Durant by his own workers! When the train he was riding to the ceremony rolled into Piedmont, Wyoming, a mob of three hundred workers—who had not been paid for several months—kidnapped him. Durant was forced to send a telegram asking that their wages be delivered so he could be freed. When the money arrived, the workers let Durant go. But they had held him long enough to make officials postpone the ceremony for two days.

morning, crews from both railroads each laid one last rail to cover the final stretch. They performed this task before a crowd of some five hundred onlookers, including railroad officials and workers, soldiers who arrived on a Union Pacific train bound for San Francisco, newspaper reporters, and other people who came to see history made.

The next part of the ceremony featured a solid gold spike, nearly 6 inches (15 cm) long and weighing 14 ounces (400 grams), which was tapped into the final rail to connect the two lines. At 12:47 P.M., when a series of speeches finally ended, Leland Stanford swung a silver **maul** to drive the golden spike home. (The spike was then extracted so it would not be stolen. Today it is displayed at Stanford University.) When the tracks were connected, the Central Pacific locomotive Jupiter and the Union Pacific Engine Number 119 pulled toward each other.

A Nation Rejoices

Telegraph wires had been attached to the spike and the hammer so that when they connected, a message would immediately be sent

The golden spike tapped into the final rail was wired to a telegraph that sent messages across the country. The spike is inscribed with names and a motto. It also has the wrong date, May 8, since the ceremony was held two days late.

Driving the Last Spike

"When they came to drive the last spike, Stanford, president of the Central Pacific, took the sledge, and the first time he struck he missed the spike and hit the rail. What a howl went up! Irish, Chinese, Mexicans, and everybody yelled with delight, 'He missed it. Yee!' Then Stanford tried it again and tapped the spike and the telegraph operators had fixed their instruments so that the tap was reported in all the offices east and west, and set bells to tapping in hundreds of towns and cities. Then vice president T. C. Durant of the Union Pacific took up the sledge and he missed the spike the first time. Then everybody slapped everybody else again and yelled, 'He missed it too, Yow!'"

Alexander Toponce, eyewitness report

The crowd gathers around for the ceremony in which Governor Stanford and Thomas Durant drove the last spike into the Transcontinental Railroad.

across the country. Even though Stanford missed and hit the tie, the historic message was relayed on the second try: "DONE!"

That one word, signifying completion of the Transcontinental Railroad, touched off a national celebration. In Philadelphia, the Liberty Bell rang; in San Francisco, 220 cannons roared; and in Chicago, tens of thousands of people marched in the city's biggest parade of the nineteenth century. People everywhere cheered, sang patriotic songs, and gathered in churches to give thanks that the great task had been accomplished.

Riding the Transcontinental Railroad

The Omaha end of the Transcontinental Railroad was linked to other railroads extending to eastern cities such as New York, thus forming a railroad covering the 3,000 miles (4,800 km) from the California coast. A trip that formerly took up to six months could now be made in seven days!

As soon as the Transcontinental Railroad was finished, passengers and **freight** began moving back and forth between the two coasts. On May 11, 1869, a passenger train headed west through Promontory Summit, while a freight train from California rumbled eastward. The trains passed each other on the single track by using **sidings** built next to the line.

About 150,000 people made the trip in the first year, and within twelve years, a million people were traveling across the country every year. So was the mail, which could now be delivered for pennies instead of dollars, as well as a steady flow of every type of product imaginable.

A Union Pacific poster (left) announces the grand opening of its railroad and route to the West from Omaha. Trains from the east coast cities would bring passengers to Omaha to connect with the Union Pacific.

All Is Changed

"A journey over the Plains was a formidable undertaking that required great patience and endurance. Now all is changed. The shriek of the locomotive wakes the echoes of the slopes along the Sierra, through the canyons of the Wasatch and the Black Hills, and his steady puffing is heard as he creeps along the mountain side. The six months journey is reduced to less than a week. The prairie schooner [a type of horse-pulled wagon] has passed away and is replaced by the railway coach with all its modern comforts."

Frank Leslie's Illustrated Newspaper, *1869*

Passenger Service

Riding the Transcontinental Railroad from Omaha to Sacramento was an affordable way to travel, but the level of comfort during the journey depended on how much people could pay for their tickets. The more travelers paid, the better their service. There were three types: first class tickets cost $100 ($1,250 today), second class $80 ($1,000), and third class $40 ($500).

First-class passengers rode in luxury and slept in Pullman cars. These sleeping cars had actual berths, like narrow bunk beds, in which people could lie down to sleep. They were fitted out with many luxuries, including steam heat when the weather was cold. Second-class passengers, however, had to sleep sitting up in padded seats, while third-class passengers were crowded into cars that had only wooden benches. Third-class cars were usually pulled by freight trains that stopped frequently and so made the trip several days longer. If there was a dining car, passengers could buy decent meals. If there was no dining car, they had to eat hurried meals whenever the train stopped at a station. There was another type of traveler as well—day passengers, people who already lived in the West but were traveling between towns. Henry Sienkiewicz, a Polish novelist who made the journey in 1876, wrote that some of these passengers were "bearded and mustached individuals dressed in ragged garments with revolvers stuck in their belts."

First-class passengers on the Transcontinental Railroad could eat in the Pullman's Palace dining cars. The cars were as comfortable as any restaurant.

This elaborate railroad car was decked out with fine furniture and fittings, including an organ. The organ is being used to play music for a religious service as the train travels across the country.

The Cost of the Railroad

The Transcontinental Railroad was the most expensive construction job undertaken in North America in the nineteenth century. The Central Pacific and Union Pacific Railroads received government loans that amounted to $64.6 million. The government also gave each railroad twenty sections (equal to 12,800 acres, or 5,200 hectares) of public land along every mile of track. In all, the two companies received 33 million acres (13 million ha). The land was valued at nearly $392 million. It was a bargain for the United States, however. When the railroads paid back the loans, the interest alone amounted to over $100 million. And although the government had given the railroads land along tracks they built, it kept every other section to sell directly to settlers who moved west. The railroads paid back nearly $170 million in loans and interest —not nearly enough to build a railroad today, but it was a vast sum then. Today, that sum would be over $2 billion.

Chapter 5

The Railroad Brings Change

The Homestead Act

In 1862, as well as signing the Pacific Railway Act, President Lincoln had signed another important new law. On May 20 of that year, he put his signature to the **Homestead** Act.

The Homestead Act helped people settle in the nation's vast middle region by offering families 160 acres (65 ha) each of free public land in western areas. By the end of the nineteenth century, the law had given 80 million acres (32 million ha) of land to about half a million farmers.

The huge growth in the western population that resulted was speeded up by the Transcontinental Railroad, which provided settlers with an easy way to get to their new homes. Soon, a giant wave of farmers, cattle ranchers, and other settlers washed across western lands. They transformed a third of the nation, previously unsettled by whites, into a region of small farming communities.

Between 1862 and 1900, thousands of families received homesteads on the condition they farmed the land for five years. Settlers, such as the family shown here in Custer County, Nebraska, left the East to claim free lands.

Railroads Create Customers

Many of the farmers and other settlers who moved west in the second half of the nineteenth century were lured there by railroads. The Union Pacific and Central Pacific wanted people to move west so they could sell them land sections along the railroad. They and other railroad companies also wanted to bring people west to ride their trains and use their services to ship farm produce to market. Railroads printed colorful posters and published pamphlets by the thousands that extolled the virtues of western land. They even sent printed material to Germany, Russia, and other foreign countries.

The increasing size of the western population paid off for the railroads. By 1880, they were getting nearly three-fourths of their revenue from people they themselves had helped moved to new homes in the West.

Millions of immigrants came to the United States from Europe in the 1800s, hoping to escape from poverty and find new opportunities. Many traveled west on the Transcontinental Railroad.

37

The Farm and Cattle Boom

The Transcontinental Railroad—and other railroads built in the West soon after—helped farmers ship corn, wheat, potatoes, and other products to markets back east more cheaply than by any other form of transportation. Without that vital link to customers, farmers could not have made a living. The opportunities opened up by the railroads also led to the creation of large cattle ranches in Texas, Arizona, Wyoming, and Colorado.

Cowboys and the Railroad

One of the most enduring symbols of the West is the cowboy, who owes a debt of gratitude to the Transcontinental Railroad. Until the railroad came, the ranchers had no way to ship beef back to hungry easterners. But the new method of transportation made it profitable for ranchers to raise huge numbers of cattle. Ranchers hired cowboys to drive their herds to **railheads** in the West, where the animals were sold and shipped directly to meatpacking plants in cities such as Chicago. The presence of the railroad created large, booming communities in railheads such as Dodge City and Abilene in Kansas.

Cowboys load cattle into a railroad car at Abilene, Kansas.

Native American People Suffer

The huge influx of new-comers onto their lands had proved disastrous for the Native peoples in eastern and far western parts of North America, where white settlement had begun more than two hundred years earlier. Now it was to destroy the homes, rights, and societies of the peoples who lived in central North America. Backed by the might of the U.S. Army, white settlers began taking land away from tribes such as the Sioux, who lived on the Great Plains. When the Native Americans fought back against the white invasion, the tribes were gradually defeated and forced by the U.S. Army to move to **reservations**.

The last tribe to resist was the Apache, and the fighting finally ended in 1886 when Apache warrior and leader Geronimo gave

For Native Americans, the coming of the Transcontinental Railroad meant the loss of land and freedom.

Driven from the Face of the Earth

"It is in vain that these poor, ignorant creatures attempt to stay [the railroad's] progress by resisting inch by inch, and foot by foot, its onward march over these lovely plains, where but a few years since they were 'monarchs of all they surveyed.' The locomotive must go forward [over] the hunting grounds of these worse than useless Indian tribes, until they are driven from the face of the Earth."

Silas Seymour, Union Pacific engineer, speaking to Congress, 1868

up. "Once I moved about like the wind," Geronimo said. "Now I surrender to you and that is all."

Broken Treaties

Soon, even the reservation land was taken away. Indian Territory, in what is now Oklahoma, was established in the 1830s as a home for tribes who had been removed from their homelands. Thousands of people from the Cherokee,

Killing the Buffalo

One way in which whites defeated Native Americans who lived on the Great Plains was to kill off the huge herds of buffalo that were the Indians' main food source. In the 1860s, an estimated 13 million buffalo roamed the Plains. By 1883, fewer than a thousand remained.

The slaughter began in earnest while the Transcontinental Railroad was being built. Hunters working for the railroads shot thousands of the animals to feed workers. One of the Union Pacific marksmen was William Cody, who won the nickname "Buffalo Bill" for shooting 4,280 buffalo in eighteen months, in 1867 and 1868.

The destruction of buffalo herds continued in the 1870s, when their hides became popular back east. Professional hunters slaughtered millions of them,

leaving the meat to rot in the sun. Passengers on the Transcontinental Railroad even shot at buffalo as their trains raced along the tracks. By 1873, western visitor Richard Dodge wrote, "Where there were myriads of buffalo the year before, there were now myriads of carcasses."

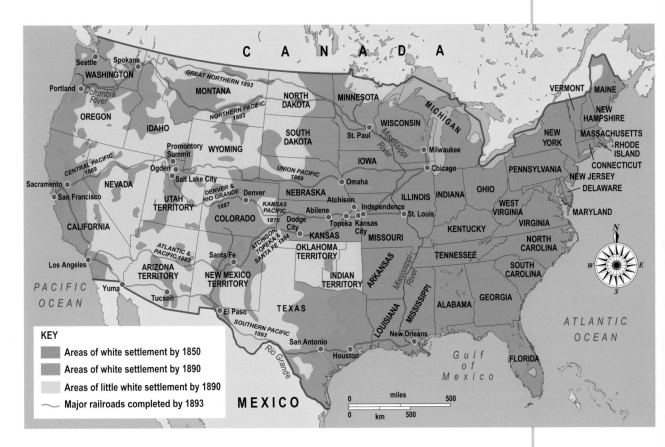

KEY
- Areas of white settlement by 1850
- Areas of white settlement by 1890
- Areas of little white settlement by 1890
- ~ Major railroads completed by 1893

Chickasaw, Muscogee, Seminole, and Choctaw tribes were forcibly banished from the Southeast by the Indian Removal Act of 1830. Against great odds, they made new homes and rebuilt their nations in Indian Territory. Later, northern and western tribes also came.

When the railroads came through in the 1860s and 1870s bringing white settlers hungry for land, the U.S. government broke treaties that said the land belonged to the Indians forever. Piece by piece, Indian Territory was opened to white settlement. In 1907, the state of Oklahoma was established, and the last remaining scrap of the much-reduced Indian Territory was no more.

More Railroads

While buffalo were being killed and Native Americans were being moved to make way for settlers flocking to the West, even more railroads were being built. By 1893, there were more railroads that reached the west coast, their tracks crisscrossing the nation in different areas. These railroads were connected to other lines, and thousands of miles of track formed a network of rail transportation that covered the entire nation.

This map shows the railroads that stretched across the West by 1893. It also shows how white settlement expanded as the railroad network grew.

41

Conclusion

Fading into History

It did not take long before the spot where the Transcontinental Railroad was completed began to fade into obscurity. In fact, as a result of inaccurate reporting of the ceremony on May 10, 1869, many people believed—and still believe—the historic event took place at Promontory Point, 35 miles (56 km) away from Promontory Summit.

Today, however, visitors can go to Promontory Summit and see the actual site where the Union Pacific and Central Pacific were joined. It is part of the Golden Spike National Historic Site, created in 1965 and run by the National Park Service.

Demise of the Train

The historic site is one of a few places where people can still see steam locomotives puffing their way along a track. In the twentieth century, the steam-powered locomotives that once roared along the Transcontinental Railroad became obsolete and gave way to newer, more efficient diesel and electric locomotives. And railroads themselves began to lose their

At Promontory Summit, Utah, replicas of the two locomotives used in the 1869 ceremony meet on the original Transcontinental Railroad track.

position as the main mode of land transportation for both freight and passengers.

In the second half of the twentieth century, airplanes, automobiles, and buses began to replace the railroad as the preferred way to travel. Although railroads still carry huge amounts of coal, grain, and chemicals over long distances, trucks now haul most of the nation's raw materials, products, and imports along highways that cross a country once ruled by the railroad.

The Legacy of the Transcontinental Railroad

Engraved on the golden spike used in the 1869 ceremony was this inscription: "May God continue the unity of our Country as this Railroad unites the two great Oceans of the world." Those simple words, written soon after the Civil War that had so divided the nation, express the importance of unity to U.S. citizens of the period. The giant construction project did, indeed, help unite the nation and cause its economy to grow. The new opportunities it brought also dramatically hastened settlement of the central part of the continent, which in turn led to a huge wave of immigration from other countries. Sadly, however, it also ensured the end of the last remaining homelands for Native people within the United States.

Time Line

1827	First railroad company is founded in United States.
1830	First railroad starts operating in United States.
	23 miles (37 km) of railroad exist in United States.
1848	United States gains large western territories at end of Mexican War.
1850	9,000 miles (14,500 km) of railroad exist in United States.
1853	March 3: Congress authorizes U.S. Army to survey possible routes for a transcontinental railroad.
1858	Butterfield's stagecoach line begins operation.
1860	More than 30,000 miles (48,000 km) of railroad exist in United States.
	Pony Express begins delivering mail.
	Theodore Judah and Daniel Strong discover a route over Sierra Nevada.
1861	Civil War begins.
	June 28: Central Pacific Railroad is incorporated.
	First transcontinental telegraph lines are completed.
	September 4: Leland Stanford is elected governor of California.
1862	May 20: Homestead Act.
	July 1: Pacific Railway Act.
1863	January 8: Central Pacific construction begins.
	October 26: First rail is laid on Central Pacific Railroad.
	November 17: Omaha, Nebraska, is selected as starting point of Union Pacific.
	December 1: Union Pacific construction begins.
1865	Civil War ends.
	July: Union Pacific construction finally moves out of Omaha.
1866	Central Pacific construction reaches Sierra Nevada.
1868	Central Pacific completes railroad through Sierra Nevada.
1869	April 28: Central Pacific workers build record 10 miles (16 km) of track in one day.
	May 1: Central Pacific and Union Pacific reach joining point at Promontory Summit, Utah.
	May 10: Ceremonial completion of Transcontinental Railroad.
1886	Apache surrender ends Indian resistance to white takeover of Native homelands.
1907	Oklahoma becomes a state and last remaining Indian Territory is abolished.
1965	July 30: Congress creates Golden Spike National Historic Site.

Glossary

anvil: iron block on which metal objects are hammered into shape. Hammering in spikes with a sledgehammer made a loud ringing sound similar to the sound of an object being struck on an anvil.

bridge monkey: worker who built train trestles.

federal: having to do with the whole nation rather than separate states.

freight: transported goods.

gandy dancer: worker who laid rails and pounded spikes into rails.

grade: make a roadbed flat and smooth.

Great Plains: area of North America between the Mississippi River and Rocky Mountains.

homestead: land acquired by settling on and farming public land instead of having to buy it.

interest: amount of extra money paid back on a borrowed sum of money.

locomotive: engine, originally steam-driven, that pulls railroad cars.

manifest: obviously true and easily recognizable. When white Americans used the phrase "Manifest Destiny," they meant it was obviously their destiny to take over the North American continent.

maul: heavy hammer.

obsolete: not needed anymore because of changed needs or because of later and more efficient inventions.

pass: low place in a mountain range; a place where it is possible to pass through a barrier or difficult obstacle.

perpetual: going on and on.

railhead: community in which the railroad begins.

reservation: public land set aside for Native American people to live on.

roustabout: worker who graded road beds.

siding: short rail track next to the main track, used as a pullout for trains.

telegraph: communication system first used in the 1800s that sends coded messages by transmitting electrical signals along wires.

topographical: having to do with the shape of the land.

train: railroad cars pulled along a track by means of animal or mechanical power.

transcontinental: crossing a continent.

trestle: braced frame of wood or metal forming a bridge to carry a railroad over a river or canyon.

Further Information

Books

Magram, Hannah Strauss. *Railroads of the West* (The American West). Mason Crest, 2002.

Moynihan, Ruth Barnes, editor. *So Much to Be Done: Women Settlers on the Mining and Ranching Frontier* (Women in the West). Bison, 1998.

Murphy, Jim. *Across America on an Emigrant Train*. Clarion, 2003.

Sita, Lisa. *Indians of the Great Plains: Traditions, History, Legends, and Life* (Native Americans). Gareth Stevens, 2000.

Stein, Conrad R. *Chisholm Trail* (Cornerstones of Freedom). Children's Press, 1998.

Winslow, Mimi. *Loggers and Railroad Workers* (Settling the West). Twenty First Century, 1997.

Web Sites

www.cprr.org Good photographs and a lot of information on a web site devoted to the building of the Central Pacific Railroad.

www.nps.gov/gosp Information about Golden Spike National Historic Site, maintained by the National Park Service; "In Depth" button leads you to a virtual tour of the park.

www.uprr.com/aboutup/history Great information about the Union Pacific Railroad and how it was built on the Union Pacific Railroad's web site.

Useful Addresses

Golden Spike National Historic Site
P.O. Box 897
Brigham City, UT 84302
Telephone: (435) 471-2209

Index

Page numbers in *italics* indicate maps and diagrams. Page numbers in **bold** indicate other illustrations.

47